In Your Nature

In Your Nature

Estlin McPhee

BRICK BOOKS

Library and Archives Canada Cataloguing in Publication

Title: In your nature / Estlin McPhee.
Names: McPhee, Estlin, author.
Identifiers: Canadiana (print) 20240533410 | Canadiana (ebook) 20240533712 | ISBN 9781771316439
(softcover) | ISBN 9781771316446 (EPUB) | ISBN 9781771316453 (PDF)
Subjects: LCGFT: Poetry.
Classification: LCC PS8625.P523 I5 2025 | DDC C811/.6—dc23

We gratefully acknowledge the Canada Council for the Arts, the Government of Canada through the Canada Book Fund, the Ontario Arts Council, and the Government of Ontario for their support of our publishing program.

Canada Council for the Arts Conseil des arts du Canada

Funded by the Government of Canada | Canada

ONTARIO ARTS COUNCIL
CONSEIL DES ARTS DE L'ONTARIO
an Ontario government agency
un organisme du gouvernement de l'Ontario

Ontario

Edited by River Halen Guri.
Author photo by Geneviève Gagnon.
The book is set in Adobe Garamond Pro.
Design by Emma Allain.

Brick Books
487 King St. W.
Kingston, ON
K7L 2X7
www.brickbooks.ca

BRICK BOOKS

Though much of the work of Brick Books takes place on the ancestral lands of the Anishinaabeg, Haudenosaunee, Huron-Wendat, and Mississaugas of the Credit peoples, our editors, authors, and readers from many backgrounds are situated from coast to coast to coast in Canada on the traditional and unceded territories of over six hundred nations who have cared for Turtle Island from time immemorial. While living and working on these lands, we are committed to hearing and returning the rightful imaginative space to the poetries, songs, and stories that have been untold, under-told, wrongly told, and suppressed through colonization.

For all my trans beloveds—
I love being in the world with you.

CONTENTS

BOY

THE DREAM JAR

In our January house, my mother
peels an apple with a knife, the skin of the peel
looping endlessly towards the table,

never once breaking. Forecast says snow.
My brother checks the red can of gasoline
is full, lingers beside his car, shoulders

hunched against the cold. My father
brings in the blankets from the garage,
puts the newspapers by the fireplace.

Three sisters with unicorn teeth
pick dreams delicately out of jars;
we all want to choose

how winter sleeps with us.
The dream horse stamps
in the room as if it were a stable,

his warm breath on the back of my neck,
asking for apples. When I wake
some years later, in a field

so far from the church
I can barely see its steeple,
I will break my teeth

on what my mother doesn't say.
My sisters will discover
their own anger; spring

will scatter us. But for now
we lay quilts over ourselves,
tuck in our kindnesses

beside our bodies. In the dream
I have plucked, I step onto the apple peel
and find snow under my feet.

I run for hours, my boots
crunching the frost, and when
I am tired, there is a grove

of apple seeds, each large enough
to climb into. Or looking for light
in the sky, I see those sharp stars

of sliced apple and my mother's hands
pinning more above me
as fast as they fall.

KEEP OUR BODIES

We were fifteen and girl-bodied, edged exquisitely in anger, gilded with it—all that gold shimmering on our beautiful boy selves like the glittering light that sometimes gathers around the moon—and we were younger, and some of us grew up. We were dandelion and horsetail, thistle and nettle, weeds snarling from hands that could never keep our bodies

gone, that never knew how to name the bodies
that were ours. We wore clothes wrong; anger
radiating from our sleeve cuffs, necklines, nettling
everywhere skin touched air. We were dazzling
tumbles of boy and girl and bird—every part of us
long and looking for flock, gathered

grey against the sky. I want us all together now. I'll gather
my ghosts—scattered around my small town, bodies
no one else can see—if you call to yours, these versions of us
still waiting to grow up. I wonder if they'll be angry
with us, if they'll recognize us. If we tell them how beautiful
they are, how beloved, will they believe us? Will it sting, nettle

on ankle—the flesh numbed where it's touched—nettle
on tongue. I don't want us to be the ones to gather
ourselves into our own arms and tell ourselves we're beautiful.
Won't someone else do that? I'm busy with words for the bodies
of birds. With *graceful, soaring.* There were no words for us,
awkward in-between, not *boy*, not *girl. Anger*

stuck, though—and *sharp*, and *shame* too. Set ablaze; anger
ignites the fire that keeps us warm. Our ghost selves nettle
their way out of the woodwork, approach the fire and us,
as we are now. I have something to say to them, gathered
around us as if we are not them. Listen: you bodies
who feel you're unwanted here—you are beautifully,

gracefully wrong. You are thistle resilient and resplendent.
Hold on to your want, weedy and determined. Let your anger
unfurl in you, becoming feathered. Your body
can name from the sky every weed below: nettle
and buttercup and mint. A whole garden, gilded. Gather
there with me like we're gathered now, the light glinting off us

brighter than a moon in the dark nettle garden, beautiful
and ours, the flame of us together gathered
into star, and our bodies worth so much grace, and anger.

DATA ON TRANSGENDER YOUTH

Huge numbers of women are justifiably terrified by the trans activists
J.K. ROWLING, "J.K. ROWLING WRITES ABOUT HER REASONS FOR SPEAKING OUT ON SEX AND GENDER ISSUES" (JUNE 10, 2020)

Turn eleven and an owl swoops in
 through your chimney with a letter

that says you're trans now—
 one of two percent, a lucky few,

chosen. You can't get out of it
 even if you're frightened by everything

you have to do on your own now,
 the words no one else understands,

the way people stare at you
 when you try to catch the train.

You've heard the stories—
 only fifty percent of people like you

have families who call them
 by the correct name.

Seventeen percent don't have anywhere
 safe to live at all.

Eight percent will be forced
 into conversion therapy.

You try to think about the happy
 parts of your life as it is now

but when you arrive at school,
 your new guardians guarantee you

a seventy-seven percent chance
          of being bullied and send you off

to learn amongst your peers.
          In between classes you dodge

every disappearing staircase
          to try to make it to the one

single-stall bathroom. Seventy percent
          of the time you just avoid

the bathroom altogether, practice
          a new kind of magic

called dehydration. When you're alone
          in the mirror you pluralize—

ten percent of those reflecting
          selves will try suicide.

Forty percent will consider it.
          The parchment of sad probabilities

unrolls at your feet, so long
          it slips under the door

and carries on into the castle,
          as though invisible.

HARMLESS

I keep my mind when I transform…I am able to curl up in my office,
a harmless wolf, and wait for the moon to wane again.
REMUS LUPIN, FROM *HARRY POTTER AND THE PRISONER OF AZKABAN* (1999)

From the moment he woke up on the train,
he was my favourite, that worn-out wolfish

brow and patched clothing. Pretty obvious
that this one liked to read, had learned

through hard knocks to be wary
and generous. I understood

what it was like to be always tired,
having stopped sleeping

to scrutinize my face in the mirror,
waiting for a change. Transformation

is something you have to do on your own,
a potion only you can take. In this singularity

we were alike: both of us mild-mannered
until we were ruthless, full-mooned

with secrets. If he was made up,
so what? I'd always had a busy imagination;

angle any shadow my way and I'd see eyes
in it somewhere. Dogs as large as dumpsters

down alleys that disappeared when I blinked.
And a different body flickering

in place of the one that belonged to me—
I could see that too, even if only for a moment

at a time. Like firelight. All that year
          I banished despair with bites of chocolate,

snapped it audibly, felt its warmth
          emanate to my toes.

It was more than just sweet, I told myself,
          it was real medicine. I told myself a lot of stories.

In my imagination, I was a boy
          moving through the forest with the ease

of an animal. If I was making myself up,
          so what?

IN 2006 EVERYONE IS TRANS—

all my friends anyway, finally;
for the first time

I'm not the only one. Together we fumble
through pronouns, parents' visits,

name changes, doctors
who need us to do their jobs for them.

We hold hands in the dining hall,
take over the bathroom

to give each other haircuts.
We try on one another's pants, trudge

weekly to the auditorium
where we watch *TransGeneration*

projected and compare ourselves
to the real people on the screen.

We do our best to forget
about family estrangements,

mandated "real life tests,"
and all that everyday bullshit.

We drive to the Beverage Den for booze;
my friends confront the cashier's glances

while I hide in the car until we're out of view
because I'm still only eighteen.

We don't sleep when we should,
me least of all. We throw ourselves

T parties, line up shots
to celebrate shots. At night

we climb out the classroom window
to see the stars from the roof,

bright enough to almost touch.
We drive to Price Chopper for chips.

We drive to Boston to use the photo booth.
One weekend we drive to Burlington,

yawning into the car at 6 AM
to get to the trans conference at 9 AM,

where we meet a hundred other trans people,
most of whom we were already aware of

from the internet. On the way home,
it's dark again. I'm in the middle

of the backseat, resting on my friend's shoulder
and us passengers tilt our heads

to see the half-filled moon
though the rear window.

My friend says something
into my hair—it no longer matters what—

and me, little insomniac, all I do
is let myself be moved forward.

AFFIRMATIONS

I brandish the love I have for you like a flame
that singes everything I touch. I am all boy
in my dreams. In my dreams, you say to my face
what you've written in every letter since time began,
which it did when you first wrote to me. I am
all boy when you look at me. I touch everything.
I say what needs to be said and then the world,
made of paper, ignites around me. I stamp
beneath my feet the hot cascade of certainty
that I should not have said what I said,
not ever, should have kept it sealed tight
in its envelope of night under my pillow.
Work is a distraction that was created just for me.
I move the mop over the dirty floor
until I am too tired to recognize the topography
of my own feelings. Am I too young for regret?
I am not too young for regret. I accept this
small-town heartbreak spooling out around me
like a threaded forest tugged from me.
Nothing crowds against me except all this space,
farmlands and fields and the arms of mountains
expanding to hold the huge sadness
that pours out of me without you here.
I drink instead of think. I attract
insomnia. I run towards the dawn, which rises
like fire over this town. I burn down
into something new.

I don't remember kissing her,
having stolen a bottle of wine

from my parents' cupboard, taken it
down to the dark river; having drunk

the whole thing, abandoned the glass
among the bracken, forgotten. Eighteen,

a warm night, sticky with stars.
Summer a desperate feeling

upon which to brush my fingertips.
Having bottled up

the idea of desire, just in case.
The trees in soft silhouette,

a moment of pavement beneath me.
Later, the hangover of a lifetime, blur

of dreamlike figures clinging
to the edges of my mind

until she finally told me
that what we were about to do

had already happened once.
Having soberly considered

that kiss an impossible option;
having once been so young

that everything was contraband,
even my own memory.

DON'T MISS THIS SHOW

That summer in the theatre
    of the mountains, acting in a body

that was mine made new, stream-
    strengthened, fed with the rush of glacial

water. Every day I walked with my world
    on my back, tended the trail brush, the loneliness

at first a thicket inside of me.
    Then each tree became itself to me

like magic. Every needle
    its own brushstroke. Surely I had always lived

here. In the clearing of buttercups,
    a black bear calm and unbothered

by us. We watched for a moment,
    then walked on. When it was dark,

it was dark. We read all the books we had
    twice over, then began to tell

our own tales. Remember
    when the rain found us—

misery and salvation. The bread
    we made each day, its rising

an act of God, a necessary
    blessing. The cougar stalking us

on our long walk back to camp.
    I wasn't always sure I would make it

out alive. One hot night we slept on the pebbly bed
    of the creek. When the full moon rose,

each of us woke as if to an alarm—
    that instant and absolute.

THE SPACE BEFORE THE THUNDER

Even this close to April there's snow and here
I am in a white dress that a woman wore
before I was born. In two hundred years
it will turn into paper and someone will use it
for the stove. All winter long

the half-sound of your voice is enough
until it isn't. We've slept so long
in a sailor's bed, stuffed with a sadness
as strong as a compass.

Tuck the dress beneath the blanket now,
as if it were me, and sing it to sleep.
Soon the summer storms will be here.
In the space before the thunder,
we count ourselves away from each other.

SEVENTEEN, LEAVING HOME

5 AM, last of August. Meet me one more time in the dead-end street
where on days without rain we lay flat against the ground, the sky
a dome above us. Our teenage cathedral, organed with towers of books,
drawing paper, strawberries. When we taught ourselves to sing
we hauled a mirror out into the road, didn't worry about breaking it,
just didn't worry. You can hear a car a mile off; there's no such thing
as smashed glass. Other days we covered the pavement in blankets,
took half-naps, studied. On dark nights when the street light burnt out,
we named the constellations to each other, mapped ourselves into them:
see, there, that creek of stars is what will carry us away,
and there, Polaris—follow my finger straight up from the Dipper—
what may bring us back home someday. Though there's no guarantee.
The lengths of all our summers fold together here like a fist.
Meet me one more time amongst the congregation of our past selves
where we stand, palms together, in what is becoming morning.

PRAYER FOR WHAT'S TO COME

You think a Christian doesn't know
about magic? Mother, your rituals:

wrap the candlesticks in cloth, twist
our wet hair into braids, bury

the birds that die. The cats
scatter those tiny graves

across the yard while you weave
a prayer like a basket

around our little bodies;
all your babies safely rocking

in the rushes. At church
we learn what the mouth is capable of,

how a sound can round a body
into an ecstatic vessel.

When you speak
in tongues, it is a spell

rolling over us on its way
to the Holy Spirit. Will it keep us

beside you as time takes
with its clever hands

the children of other people
and turns them into strangers?

After all, Jesus came back
from the dead; the cross

on its gold chain is an amulet
you wear to summon the possibility

of return. Mold us in his image,
that we may withstand the test

of the wilderness, and be granted
the final flourish of resurrection.

There is nothing torn asunder
that God can't put right.

Maybe one day you will make us
into such magicians.

WOLF

LYCANTHROPY

Metaphor begets metaphor. A man
is a beast, a messenger

from God, a thing you'll never be.
A forest, an ocean. A needle

is a supernatural ability.
A wolf is a wildness, is mythological

transformation, is affliction.
A not-doing is TV static stuck

in your chest. Danger begets
something desperate, like teeth

growing from the ground—
lily of the valley with fangs

instead of flowers. A bouquet
is a beckoning, is a parenthood,

is a weeping. A boy is waiting
by the edge of the woods

for whatever comes next.

TURNING

Through the half-window you track
daylight rising and falling, the moon
          an eraser mark

in the smudge of afternoon. In the church
basement the other kids want to burn
          Harry Potter—incendiary,

absurd. Is this my life,
a voice inside you wants to know
          and when the answer comes

you cannot go back
to what you were. Mirrors shatter
          in your wake; walls grow

fur, grow forest. Limbs
lengthen, gangling. Hearts
          harden. Even Jesus turns

his face away, won't speak with you.
You who are some other creature, perhaps
          the only one of your kind, genderless

and ravenous, running
from God's house, glossolalia
          vanishing from your tongue,

which rolls back
into what it once was, shriveled
          into seed. In this wilderness

you scrabble for a foothold and find it
as though you have always been clawed,
          bestial. The trees teach you.

In this way you become a stranger
to yourself. You become
          yourself, stranger.

WOLF'S BANE

Even a man who is pure in heart and says his prayers by night may become a wolf when the wolfbane blooms and the autumn moon is bright.
FROM *THE WOLF MAN* (1941)

Raised to be afraid
of everything, especially

men, dark places   Especially burning

forests and aconite
witchcraft   And no wonder

More than myth
to say God bears a million

names, faces   In the strange mirror

splitting heaven   from what's below it

the devil does too—
likeness and antidote

Hard to know   which is which
when you spin

on the spot   for so long

trying to find
your way

GAY MESSIAH

We all have our little rebellions. I, for instance,
cut off my hair and take up witchcraft,

will chant anything sublunary
or otherwise to summon other queers

to my small town. Primarily they materialize
from old books, their outlines smudgy,

their clothing outdated. Resurrected
and exhausted, they are busy

with their own dramas and don't want to talk
to me. Shakespeare is here, mingling

with Artemis, who won't stop fiddling
with her arrows. Turns out even the godliest

among us has something to prove
to their parents. At the party

in my mind, I'm in charge for once
so Jesus is here, is queer,

and looks eerily similar
to Rufus Wainwright. He slouches

at the piano, playing songs
he learned from the dead.

Emo, yes, but you work with what you've got.
I sit on the thick carpet in my brother's

hand-me-downs and sing along, entranced
by the new outline of my skull,

that lightness like a halo. By midnight
we're all holding hands, flesh

and ghost. Jesus brings out a cauldron,
travel-size, and lights up

a fire in it, tells us to burn
what no longer serves us.

Where to start? I turn out my pockets.
And will I have anything

left after? Jesus stops in front of me.
Your turn, he says. My turn.

LOVE WON OUT

The sin of homosexual behavior, like all sins, can be forgiven and healed by the grace revealed in the life and death of Christ.
LOVE WON OUT: CONFERENCE GUIDE (2005)

gay and gangly when the internet was new
scrolling through gender
all summer long
possible selves draped over the bed
like back-to-school outfits
I step into boy jeans and skate shoes
kick off junior year by starting the Gay-Straight Alliance
crying in the bathroom
I've only ever seen another trans person
on the screen
I delete my history
badly
my mother orders a boxful of dark green pamphlets
from Focus on the Family
ex-gay propaganda
for your friends in your group
she says
all year the pamphlets appear in my room
I make them vanish
silently

ONE DIRECTION

This cup is the new covenant in my blood, which is poured out for you.
LUKE 22:20

One can't simply waltz
out of the Pentecostal church

without first internalizing
the fundamental tenet

For God so loved the world
he created five-piece boy bands

that regenerate every decade
O stylish saviours of dusty summers

and long car rides *Let's pray*
we stay young

stay made of lightning
Sunday school stacks of verses

I memorized in exchange for gold stickers
but I see now I may have misunderstood

the original assignment
Love is patient

love is kind of like
being the way that you are is enough

I only want to love what I love
with new joy

Let's *have a celebration*
the music up the windows down

I was born this way
Evangelism helixed into my make-up

before I could try
to pretend to be someone else

Have you heard the good news
Opportunities for gospel abound

when one breaks
with restrictive definitions of divinity

Now God speaks to me
through any number of sacrilegious subjects

and I listen
In the beginning was the Word

and the Word was
written in these walls

I was always going to have to leave
the church though there remains in me

a sanctuary and the Lord
who is my shepherd

leads me beside still waters and then
makes me over in his image

a tiny temporary star
catapulting through boyhood

where *there's nothing to be afraid of*
even when the night changes

THE GOSPEL OF LUKE

The only book in which you'll find them
in this tableau, the younger sitting at the foot

of the Lord, listening. Tiny footnote. Mary
—same name as so many other women he kept

around him at that time; hard to say who she was,
truly. Not a cook, nor much of a cleaner,

it seems, not according to her sister,
anyway. Poor old Martha, left to make and serve

dinner, host the guests, bake the bread. Whirling
around like a tired top, all those disciples

to feed. All that mud on the floor.
When she asked the famous teacher (you know,

Jesus Christ) to tell Mary to help her
and his only response was, *"Mary has chosen*

what is better," I wouldn't have blamed her
for whatever she did. But the story ends

there. I assume Jesus was served his meal,
that Martha cleaned up after, gave them all

a place to sleep. Continued to care
for her sister—the more brilliant mind,

of course. I expect Jesus just forgot
to tell the parable of Martha afterwards,

how work is a form of prayer, and no one
starves when your praying is the kind

that makes dinner appear on the table.
Too busy walking on water, perhaps.

Surely everyone wants a man
with a miracle up his sleeve.

JESUS WEPT

Now a man named Lazarus was sick. He was from Bethany, the village of Mary and her sister Martha. This Mary, whose brother Lazarus now lay sick, was the same one who poured perfume on the Lord and wiped his feet with her hair. So the sisters sent word to Jesus, "Lord, the one you love is sick."
JOHN 11:1-3

And now for a counting of the miracles.
Each a performance of transformation,

as a silk handkerchief changes
colour under the hand's quick stroke.

Let's start with the fun stuff: at the party
that no one wanted to stop, Jesus

turned the water to wine—thank
God, things were getting tense.

After that, it was easy to multiply
two fishes and some old loaves

into food for thousands, attracting applause
(how *did* he do it?) and the state's

watchful eye. He healed the sick, of course;
that's a basic requirement for any saviour

and luckily for him very hard to quantify.
He gifted his name to countless generations

of water bugs, striding on the surface
of those waves like he was just

out for an evening stroll, a definite
crowd-pleaser. Still, everyone was waiting

for the big showstopper.
Martha and Mary had hoped

he would use the time he had left
to save Lazarus, their brother,

whom he loved. But he dithered—
precious time passed and so did Lazarus,

dead in the tomb for four days
before Jesus finally stopped by.

Oh, the tears he cried! Famous enough
to turn to slang two thousand years later.

After weeping his holy heart out,
he sprang into action, ordered the stone

rolled away from the tomb. Martha,
always practical, protested

that the stench would be too great.
But Jesus had his response ready:

"Did I not tell you that if you believed,
you would see the glory of God?"

So the sisters briefly became his assistants
and set up the final reveal. Then,

his greatest miracle, as he called the dead man
to rise, come out. And Lazarus rose;

he returned to us. What a curtain call.
None of us were the same after.

MARTHA AND MARY WITNESS JESUS'S DEATH ACROSS TIME AND SPACE

AUGUST

I find the man in the forest behind our house,
the gashes on his back stuck with blood
and the long grass. I holler for my sister

and she comes running
as if the dog were down the well.
We're not the kind to ask too many questions

so we just carry the man home, lay him gingerly
on the fold-out bed in the living room.
It's already August; the heat

pulls a sweat out of him.
My sister sits with him, keeps the cloth
on his forehead damp. He asks for blackberries

so I go out to the edge of town, dusk
just beginning, and return with a bucketful,
so sweet the taste of one is enough

to take the last hurt out of him.
It leaves him looking as though he's been splashed
all over with light

and for years afterwards the neighbours swear
he got up from the couch,
walked out into the street

and right up to heaven. Leaving behind
the pail of blackberries
beside the stove, my palms

stained red with their juice,
and the new jam lined up on the counter,
dark and viscous in the glass jars.

We give jam to all the neighbours
and they say it must have been blessed
by the Lord, it tastes that good.

MARTHA AND MARY WITNESS JESUS'S DEATH ACROSS TIME AND SPACE

WOLF

As a child my grandmother learned to be careful
at Christmas and then at Easter, when the shape
of the wolf hinged open like a jaw,

shifted men into itself, so that they became
that grotesque in-between thing,
both man and beast. The souls

of the afflicted saved only by driving nails
through their hands. In my own childhood,
the wolf comes out of the forest,

dragging its back legs along the ground,
and collapses, shuddering, in front of a quickly
gathering crowd. Above us, a white moon.

It's plain to see the wolf is dying
but my father shoots it anyway, shaky
aim failing to put an end

to its life. Its eyes pale, polished stones.
The wolf's ribs heave with a human despair,
its breathing as fast as a heart.

Its mouth snaps open at nothing.
Of all the things I have seen die, none
have been so pitiful as this. The creature

looked down upon by the crescent
of our well and waiting bodies.
It turns its slow eyes to my younger sister,

who moves forward as though enchanted
to sit beside its teeth. The wolf pulls its body
towards her and lays its head on the skirt

I finished for her just yesterday,
liquid from its mouth staining the wool.
All around us the night heavy as winter.

A terrible rasping breath and suddenly
the wolf is still. Then lying with his head
on my sister's skirt is a man, naked and strange

to me, his side bleeding and red wounds
on his hands. My sister goes on stroking the dead hair.
My grandmother crosses herself,

says, *Lord, forgive us,* but I don't know
if she means for the killing of the wolf
or for having a man of such monstrosity among us.

MARTHA AND MARY WITNESS JESUS'S DEATH ACROSS TIME AND SPACE

SNOW

The forest keeps things
dark. Without the stars we might have stumbled

right over him. His body at our feet
like an awkward bird knocked from flight.

My sister keeps hold of my hand
with the tiniest monkey fingers.

The man is lying naked
in the snow. I would say dead

except his breath wisps through the cold air.
Dying, then. Blood smeared on his side

as if someone laid a baby's red blanket over him.
My sister tugs me down, our knees soaking,

and we look into his face. For a second, maybe,
he looks at us too. Eyes spark

and extinguish. Then we blink
and the body is gone, as if it had never been there.

The only thing before us is a warm depression
in the snow and the blanket of blood.

I touch it to make sure it's real.

LUPO MANNARO

Nonna, hurtling into her twentieth year,
tucks herself into a train that scampers four-legged

over Italy, leaves a year behind
in a refugee camp—changeling child,

could be anyone. Turns out to be
just who she is. Sharp-witted, sweet

as swallowing a comet. She spins
in the mirror until it's time to clamber aboard

the ocean, its long cold trail spitting her
into another train, which zooms in slow motion

all the way across Canada to a city
where she knows no one. A wolf

is a wolf wherever it's from
unless you call it by a different name

and then it is exactly what it is.
When she unlatches her suitcase

in her new language, the trinkets
from home spring out like a pop-up book,

scattering into the forest
around her. Someone else's life

is a story if that's what you say it is.
She zips herself into a new tongue,

drops crumbs of her old Fiuman
to follow back to herself later, droops

to sleep while night elbows
itself into the frame. The narrator

sews together cautionary folktales
as needed. Nonna, remember—

if you sleep outside, cover your face
to keep away the moon, strange predator.

Refuse excommunication. Don't turn
into something else.

But she can't hear through the thick glass
of time between us. All those old wives' tales

told too late, Nonna transforms
into an old woman, or at least that's how she appears

to me now. When I squint
to see the girl as she must have been,

ghostless and peering forward
into the future as she swims by herself

off the cliffs in the bright Adriatic,
I see her in black and white.

ROMULUS AND REMUS

Twins tucked into a basket, set afloat
on the river,   dreaming of Moses

or maybe of another story
altogether.   Tiberinus, god

who could have drowned them,
delivered them   to their new mother

the wolf. Twins suckling
like pups   at the mouth

of the river that birthed them
into new   creatures. Loping

into boyhood in the pastures,
tending sheep,   growing

teeth. Raised to be shepherds
howling   into adolescence

without memory of that first furred
warmth.   Lineage obscured

twice over, parentage godly,
royal   or beastly.

Of all these, is it the wolf
we should fear?   Animal—

villain in the tales
we tell.   Another story:

how it would have been
if they had stayed   quiet

in the cave of their childhood,
limited   their ambitions.

Never arrived at the crossroads
of their dispute,   the inability

to remain two. Twins
tugging   in different directions

until one vanquished
the other,   victorious to be

the killer, not the killed.
To alone   be the teller

of the story. And the city
that sprang out   of the telling—

empire and law, gods and priests;
twinning,   wolfing up the landscape.

GENESIS

The witch created the werewolf.
            On her way to commune
                        with the devil,

flight-giving unguent in hand,
            she cursed the man before her—
                        covered him

in that same ointment,
            which contorted his limbs,
                        transformed his body, destroyed

his mind. Centuries of trials
            in which the wolf bounded
                        alongside the accused witch,

a perverse kind of familiar,
            feral. Cowering in her shadow.
                        Or sometimes she and he

were one and the same,
            charged with all
                        the usual evils—

fraternizing with Satan, self-
            delusions. Who let this terror
                        into the world?

Painted each hair one by one, crook'd
            each tooth. Who designed
                        the grasses

gathered into broom? Who dreamt up
            the forest, filled with perfect
                        tinder?

And who lit the match.
The witch created the werewolf—
who created the witch?

FOREST

TEEN WOLF

I'm not a fag. I'm a...werewolf.
SCOTT HOWARD, FROM *TEEN WOLF* (1985)

City bricked with night
shadows, dim little moons
above the alley entrances,
barely enough light to make out
the new angles of your face,
your hand in mine. We're changing.
Separately—your muscles
thickening, voice deepening—
and together, as we shift closer
to each other's body, taking
on the feeling of the other. In love,
one acquires an extra sense;
some of what you taste
makes it to my mouth, too.
Our shadows behind us
like one animal strolling
the empty street. The truck
that screams past is a warning
shot meant to frighten us
away. "Fags!" shouted
from the window, howl
of tires. What kind
of boys are we to them?
Dangerous monsters.

TRANSVECTION OF A NEW KIND

The werewolf is neither man nor wolf, but a satanic creature with the worst qualities of both.
DR. YOGAMI, FROM *WEREWOLF OF LONDON* (1935)

The Greyhound beams its headlights
through southern Oregon's deep night,
moonless. Dry trees looming, unseen
tinder on the other side of the cold,
cracked window. I lean my newly shorn head
against the dirty plastic, try to sleep.
Two in the morning the bus puffs to a stop
and a white guy in a red ball cap
slams down in the seat next to me. Turns
to me and says, "Are you a boy or a girl?"
He takes out his lighter, flicks it into flame
next to my knee. Closes it again.
"Do you fuck girls?" Snick of fire
near my leg before it extinguishes.
I conspire and appease, stay seated,
stay awake. Hours later the sky sends up
its own blaze and the bus clinks him out
at a stop in California. I exhale. Whoever I was
before stares at me from the blurry window
and I stare back, imperceptibly altered.

THE LOOKING GLASS

I've always seen you this way—
the way you are: fractal, crystal
sharp and refractive. Even
in college when you tumble
in my window and I marvel
at my good luck. To find
another witty fairy, someone
like me who shimmers
with discomfort but obscures it
better. I know you're a girl
because you'll never believe
you're easy to love.
We take pictures in mirrors,
disappear into fiction
and opposite coastlines, inverts
of each other. We are both
former small town Jesus freaks
freaking out in the big city.
Long before it's common practice,
we video call each other
every few months. I feel
protective and weird
when everyone wants
to Zoom all the time—
that's our thing. And I hate
seeing myself on the screen.
Except when it's with you,
all those years of staring
at the borders where our faces
meet, meld. Some things change,
some things don't.

BOY

i.

That tug between bodies that moves my mouth
like a bridle. You weren't what I thought

would pull me. But then neither of us the boy
the other expected. Boys to me are shapeshifters,

familiars, beloved. Like the boy in the mirror—
shadow who is so like me

except that he can leave when he needs to,
turn himself into tree branch

or disappear down the long corridor
within my own reflection.

ii.

I've always been like this, mutable,
wordless. Inside of body, *boy*

asserts itself. Inside of that
are things I never knew

about myself. I'm capable of loving
people who are not trans,

attempting legibility within the palimpsest
of self through time. Boyhood

shaped you into a closed book
and me into open scaffolding.

iii.

I remember what you smelled like when you were a stranger.
I had a dream then in which we stood together

in a field. What comes to me now still in colour
is how, standing, we held each other

and you were quiet in my ear when you said you loved me—
I woke and remembered everything

I didn't know about you.
That first month you lay bare-chested before me

and I expected to see scars, their soft lines
phantom under my hands.

iv.

Boy a set of nesting dolls—crack open
that syllable to another, hidden sonant;

a door that leads to doors, rooms
that accordion out of themselves.

Or a maze and the signs
that lead us out again.

v.

It’s never been a question of love.
Remember that ferry ride we took back

from the island? I left you briefly
and then returned. When I came back,

you were looking through the panorama
of windows while we moved over the ocean.

The sight of you surrounded
by blue dismantled me.

YOUNG HEARTS RUN FREE

At work, I talk about suicide with teenagers
over and over until the word loses meaning,
scrambles itself with *sluice* in my head—
a recurrence of teenagers, a sluice of suicide.
Sometimes they never return to see me
and then the computer flickers like a neon cross,
blank and bright. Fireworks rocket over the city
as though we have something to celebrate.
After work, I drop my body into the ocean,
let something larger than myself hold me up.
Every day is another decade since I was a teenager.
Eventually the sluice runs so strong
that I take time off work to stop thinking
about teenagers killing themselves.
At home, I watch a Norwegian TV show
about teenagers over and over and weep
extravagantly. On the blinking blue of the screen,
Norwegian teenagers watch *Romeo + Juliet*,
then kiss under water. Somewhere without me
my teenagers muddle through. Or they don't.
At night, they dart into my dreams like arrows,
always something in their hands—a bottle,
a needle, a knife. Somewhere else in time
my teenage self watches *Romeo + Juliet*
over and over until I am electric blue, weeping
like a kettle. We are all made of dust. This year
the number of those who return to dust
is astronomical. Every day is a deluge
since my own teenagehood. We think we know
how this ends, but every time it feels different.

MARTHA AND MARY WITNESS JESUS'S DEATH ACROSS TIME AND SPACE

BRIDGE

We walk along the bank of the dirty river,
our backs to the forest that shrinks every year.
My sister runs ahead of me, picking up
the shards of glass that have smashed ashore,
even though I tell her not to, every time. She stops,
eyes caught on something in the skyline. *Look*, she says,
pointing at the arch of the bridge in the distance. I look.
There's a figure poised on the edge, too far to hear us.
Stop, I scream into the wind anyway. He doesn't listen,
falls like water pouring—one fluid movement—
and then the light tricks me and his body flashes
into a bird shape, pulling itself up and away
from the river. The vision lasts a second;
when I look again there is no body, only the water
moving as it always moves. And my sister
staring at where the man was a moment ago,
current lapping over her toes, as though
there is something there only she can see.

GLOSSOLALIA

And these signs will accompany those who believe: In my name they will drive out demons; they will speak in new tongues
MARK 16:17

Jesus didn't save me but my grandmother did
RAE SPOON, "I CAN'T TEAR IT FROM ME"

i. *Epifania*

Having seen the star proclaiming the birth of Jesus,
the Magi set out to find the newborn king.
Along the way, they invite the hag Befana

to accompany them but she refuses,
as she has too much sweeping to do.
After they leave, she changes her mind,

climbs aboard her broomstick to follow—
but she's too late! To this day she searches,
leaving gifts for children on the eve of Epiphany,

hoping one of them is the child whom she seeks.

ii. *The First Manifestation of Christ*

My mother. Warmth and flannel when she called us
to her, all our little bodies in nightgowns
she'd made, gold thread edging soft pink fabric.

She combed and braided our hair,
tucked us in and turned out the light,
told us, *If the devil comes near you,*

just tell him to leave in Jesus's name,
and he will. In that open space
of my imagination he bloomed, split himself

into shadow, smoke, pinpricks of eyes
that at any moment might flash fire. My own eyes
wide open, as if offering my sight was enough

to ward off what I didn't want to see.

iii. *Perception of the Essential Nature*

My nonna. Polished shells and framed photographs
on the mantelpiece, the bathroom counter, the bedroom
vanity. Her mother a beautiful spectre in black and white

next to the oval mirror, dead already
by the time my nonna was five. Rosary
wrapped around the bedpost. Memories of her mother

swatches of what could have been—
the pressure of being held, perfume.
I remember when my nonna held my hands

and told me a story of visions. After her mother's death,
she saw pupils on the insides of her eyelids,
someone else's eyes imprinted over her own

bright ones. How that scared her, demon-
fearing, so like her daughter in that way.
My mother, who left the cathedral

of her mother's belief and baptized herself anew
into the church of tongues. Glossolalia
is a language that one neither learns nor loses;

it's simply given to you, remains in the body.

iv. *Manifestation of a Divine Being*

In my mind's eye, I conjure the sight of my nonna's
Christmas living room: the tree decked silver with tinsel,
the carpet forest-soft underfoot. *Crostoli*

—angel wings—in the tin on the table,
dusting our fingers in powdered sugar,
snowprints left across the illustrated

pages of the only storybooks in her house. Strega Nona's
spaghetti pot; Befana flying on her broomstick,
trailing just behind those wise men

in her search for the holy child. Call it apparition
—*apparizione*—or manifestation, the end result
is the same: belief becomes a body. As if

in the moment Jesus was seen for the first time
he became himself, unghosted
into his power. How I waited for him

to come storming in and banish every demon
I'd ever believed into existence. My mother
was frightened out of Catholicism

by the stories of the devil the nuns spun.
Had my nonna known sooner, she told me,
she would have swept right in and held her

little body safe, wrapped in wool and flannel.

v. *Illumination*

She can teach you how to search—
unrelenting, ever hopeful. Leaving gifts
in your wake as you circle and recircle

the legacy of what is unknown
yet somehow also known. *Epifania*.
Strega. The woman who flew away

from everything she knew
because God compelled her.
She sweeps each floor before she takes flight again.

She travels the night, unafraid of demons.
She twists dough into angels' wings.
She braids her children's hair with gold thread.

She speaks every language.

RIGHTEOUS BUTCH

I did not put on men's clothing by the counsel of any man on earth. I did not put on this clothing, nor do anything else, except at the bidding of God and the angels.

JOAN OF ARC, ON TRIAL FOR HERESY IN 1431

Every other month I pored over
an illustrated children's book
about Joan of Arc from the library,
transfixed by her lit-up form.
She looked like a boy; she was
on fire. She talked to trees, could hear
the Lord's crystalline articulation.
Ancestor of craft, cross-dressing
her way to the stake, first burnt
then beatified. I loved her short hair,
her conviction. Righteous
butch and teenage martyr
without the ability to choose
the words used for her body. *Witch*,
they called her, then *Saint*.
I knew the meaning of both,
though not how they could be paired
until she taught me. Duality
tempered in flame, the world
smithed into a different light.
The kindling of her paper-
white dress. Now there is
no separation, only crackling
magic and new gender. As for me,
I did nothing except at the bidding
of God and the angels.

TURNING BACK

To test your power you return
to the megachurch of your childhood,
          tiny knife tucked into the body

of the cross swinging from your gold
necklace, little flash
          of protective glamour.

You cross the threshold into the familiar house
of worship—cavernous, brimming
          with LEDs—and become a pillar of salt,

as you always knew you would.
How many times did they warn you
          not to look back?

Now your body made of salt runneth over,
decorating the new carpets with fine grit.
          No one notices you've changed;

the woman in front of you turns around
to hold your briny hands, declares you beautiful
          in the eyes of God. She was born

again forty-nine years ago. On stage
there's an earnest attempt at a soft rock concert
          in the name of Jesus.

Your crumbling arms
place the miniature plastic communion cups
          into their miniature cup holders

attached to the back of the seat in front of you.
The pastor is lacklustre, offers up,
          "Forgive my sins—

I repent, I turn from them,"
while the cheap grape juice crystallizes
    on your tongue. He fails

to share any delicious details, spares you
talk of condemnation,
    which you strangely miss.

You can't help it—it's in your nature
to look for a bit of Sodom
    and Gomorrah.

It's easier to be made of salt
than you thought it would be
    when you were younger.

Most of you remains in your body.
After it's over, you return
    to your whole life.

HUMAN NATURE

The lake a basin of fog with the moon dropped into it.
Us on the dock, breaking silence into quarters

with our silhouettes—poised, conjuring
night thick on our shoulders like a mist

stole. August rolling towards its own end,
though I'd been in the forest long enough

by then to forget the date. You remembered:
it was Michael Jackson's birthday.

You were shouting a sort of tribute
into the darkness; all night you'd been waiting

to dance for the occasion, one hand
flashing up silver out of shadow. Reaching out

to touch a stranger, as it were. Orion's Belt
sparkling on the invisible horizon.

Even unseen we could feel it fastening
us into our hemisphere, where all week

we'd been trying to reconstruct that old myth,
to figure out the truest version of events

and who was to blame. Orion in the water
with Artemis's arrow flying towards him

out of his own making or else the scorpion
at his heel: jealousy, justice, hubris, shame—

we'll never know what it takes for a person
to turn into a constellation. All we can say for sure

is that no matter how you spin the tale,
it ends the same. Or begins. Someone,

somewhere, looking out across the nighttime.
So what if sometimes we want

to be the kind of story someone else would tell.
I hope they get it right, that they remember

the details. Like how long we kept ourselves in the rain
for the possibility of a kiss. Your dress

a sheet of starlight over the black lake.
How midnight smudged the woods around us

into velvet and softened all the clocks.
I know there's too much injustice in our own time

to worry over what went wrong
thousands of years ago, so why are we so angry

about what's passed. Like hearsay
and the chances we never got. If they say why,

why, tell them I don't want to lose
to history, love distorted

or buried by time and our own fearful mythologizing
of what really happened. Looking out

across the moment, I can say with certainty
that I would have stood there shaking

in the chill to hear you sing
until morning burst onto the scene

and sent all the constellations running.
So what if music is just the sound

of what's already burnt out
piercing like new every time it alights

around the dark of your body.
I still liked when you'd *hee hee* higher

than I'd ever heard anyone go and then fall
into laughter. Both of us arrow-bright

and buoyant as gems. There was a ridge of stars
we were waiting to become.

CONSTELLATION

There we are, June gloom settling, a glitter
of metal dangling from your ear.

We wind our way downtown to the show,
tired and untouching. Trying to have a good time.

I can picture Orion at home in Los Angeles,
making himself a star. Greek nose. A hunter

comfortable in that wilderness.
See him strutting through the hazy heat

to the crystal shop, where I buy a nugget
of green tourmaline, tuck it into my pocket

for later, its supposed heart
energy bursting through the seams,

threadlight. We follow the signs
to the Walk of Fame because I asked you

to take me there, and you do. A sky of smooth
famous names under my feet; as above,

so below. And you and me—
we've changed

but are still kind to each other.
I lay the green-threaded crystal

on a coral star and we send our laughter
out through time and space.

PRAYER FOR OUR PAST SELVES

Dear friends, since God so loved us, we also ought to love one another.
I JOHN 4:11

This year your birthday happens in absence
while I am looking back
over my shoulder at our two figures,
feet sunk in the mud of the river bank.
Lord, whatever you are, scatter
language over me like salt.
I'm trying to find a way to tell
those kids that they won't become
who they think they will—
people more extraordinary than us.
They'll simply carry on being themselves.
Days move us closer to more days
until there is a catalogue of mornings behind us
and we are done. This year
a friend dies on my birthday
and I go to the water to say goodbye,
though he is not at the water,
not even in this city. Lord,
wherever you are, help me
make this strange translation
through time. That now an ocean
away from you I am still a body
who is part of the world. Night falls
as green as cedar, shaking us
into sudden forests. Some days we wake up lost.
Lord—you who are nothing—
what words could there be
to assure those old selves?
They only want to be certain
that we will always be
in the same place to celebrate
crocus and equinox, blackberry,
birthday. Some days we are full

of birdsong. Lord, nothing
is as certain as this. They know
what we know now. It may be
that they were the ones who told us.
The grey rush of the river
a moving mirror at our feet.
Of course it will wash away.
All that has been and everything else
besides. Whatever you are,
you can count on that. Even so—
if you're listening, Lord, and all the more
if you're not—I have a prayer
I'd like to say. Bless the young
people who were us; bless us.
Together, and apart.

WHAT LOVE CAN'T DO

It's this endless orchestral ache, like the bow
never lifts from the violin strings. The note held taut.

You, transplant, no matter what city or song.
The enormity of what I wish

I could offer you an ocean streaming from my hands.
I will love you across all landscapes,

across names, pronouns, your shape shifting
or not. I'll love you so much

that something will heal—the scars
you didn't choose smoothed back into skin.

The scars you did choose worn to the beach.
Let's take them swimming.

I will love you enough
that you'll be able to walk into the water again,

the way you haven't in years, salt crash
and tug on your body. How long has it been?

Since you were so young
you could have been swept away by the tide.

I will love you until the tide changes
and we're all swept backwards—

your mother calling you into the house
instead of telling you to leave it.

NOTES

All quoted passages from the Bible are taken from the New International Version (NIV); in particular, I referenced my childhood Bible, which contains the original translation of the NIV published in 1978. The NIV has since been revised twice, in 1984 and 2011, but I've kept the original wording here for consistency and in keeping with what I grew up reading.

DATA ON TRANSGENDER YOUTH

The statistics are from the following sources:

- Darcy Hango and Elena Prokopenko, "Bullying victimization among sexually and gender diverse youth in Canada" (2022)
- Soren Hodshire, "Understanding the Transgender Portion of Our Population" (2023)
- Trans PULSE Canada, "QuickStat#1 — Conversion Therapy" (2019)
- Trans PULSE Canada, "Health and well-being among trans and non-binary youth" (2021)

TURNING

In 1999, *Harry Potter* was denounced by Focus on the Family for witchcraft. The book series continues to be a central figure in the conversation on evangelical book bans and book burning, while also more recently coming under scrutiny by queer and trans people for the author's repugnant and relentless transphobia.

WOLF'S BANE

Wolfsbane is also known as aconite (and monkshood, among other names), and is a real and very poisonous plant that has folkloric werewolf-fighting properties. In extremely small doses it has been used as a medicinal cure for aches, pains, and fevers, though please note it is very, very poisonous. This poem attempts to reflect that duality in its shape, which is that of a mirror, split halfway across the center.

GAY MESSIAH

The title of this poem is taken from a Rufus Wainwright song, which first appeared on the EP *Waiting on a Want* and then on his fourth studio album *Want Two*, both in 2004.

LOVE WON OUT

Love Won Out was an ex-gay ministry run through Focus on the Family from 1998 to 2009 and then through Exodus International from 2009 to 2013, when Exodus International was disbanded. John Paulk, the founder of Love Won Out, apologized for the harm he and his ministry caused and now identifies (again) as a gay man. Alan Chambers, the CEO of Exodus International, formally apologized on behalf of the organization for the damage caused by conversion therapy and other aspects of the ex-gay ministry.

ONE DIRECTION

Inspired by Luke 22:20, in which Jesus offers wine as a manifestation of his blood to his disciples, red letter edition Bibles print in red ink all the words considered to have been spoken by Jesus. Because we were unable to print in red, red letter text is instead represented throughout the book by grey Zondervan font, which is used in many NIV Bibles. In this poem, the lines in Zondervan are lyrics from One Direction songs.

THE GOSPEL OF LUKE

Luke 10:38-42 is the only place in the Bible with this story of Martha and Mary, which is often interpreted as a reminder to not get caught up in worldly tasks and miss out on Jesus's teachings as a result. I have always had a soft spot for Martha, whose work is so resoundingly dismissed, and the series of persona poems of her and her sister Mary witnessing Jesus's death grew out of my curiosity over who she could have been.

JESUS WEPT

It's unclear whether the Martha and Mary that feature in the Gospel of Luke are the same Martha and Mary of Bethany, who count Lazarus as their brother, but for my purposes here they are. John 11:35 ("Jesus wept.") is famous for the being the shortest verse of the Bible in the King James Version and has been given new life as a contemporary expletive.

ROMULUS AND REMUS

In Roman mythology, the founding of the city of Rome begins with twins Romulus and Remus, who are born into a complicated tangle of political tensions that result in them being left to die in the river Tiber. From there, the she-wolf (or lupa) cares for them before their adoption into a shepherding family. Eventually their royal fate catches up with them and, later down the line, they compete to found a major city, culminating in a quarrel in which Remus is killed and Romulus founds the city of Rome. Romulus and Remus are commonly depicted in art as babies nursing from the body of the lupa.

GENESIS

There are numerous versions of how the folkloric relationship between werewolves and witches came to be; one tale holds that werewolves were created out of a witch's curse. Regardless, werewolf trials were held throughout the 15th-18th centuries in Europe, alongside the witch trials. In many places, lycanthropy was associated with magic, which had direct connections to Satan, so to be accused of being a werewolf was often a de facto accusation of being a witch.

YOUNG HEARTS RUN FREE

This poem takes its title from the 1976 Candi Staton song, which was covered by Kym Mazelle for Baz Luhrman's *William Shakespeare's Romeo + Juliet* in 1996. Harold Perrineau as Mercutio performs a brief but unforgettable sequence in drag to this song in the film.

RIGHTEOUS BUTCH

In 1431, Joan of Arc was put on trial in front of a pro-English ecclesiastical court, found guilty of heresy, and burned at the stake. Centuries later, she was canonized as a saint. The first unabridged English translation of the transcript of her trial, *The Trial of Jeanne d'Arc*, was published in 1932 by W.P. Barrett. In 1936, Willard Trask compiled an "autobiography" entitled *Joan of Arc: Self-Portrait*, which translated and assembled direct statements about her life from letters and the trial transcript into a chronological narrative. The epigraph of this poem is taken from Trask's work, from Joan of Arc's trial transcript on February 27, 1431.

HUMAN NATURE

This poem takes its title from the Michael Jackson song of the same name, which appeared on his sixth solo album, *Thriller* (1982). Several lines quote or reference the lyrics.

ACKNOWLEDGEMENTS

Thank you to everyone at Brick Books for the most supportive and rewarding publishing experience I could have ever imagined. River Halen is the editor I have always dreamed of working with: perceptive, imaginative, incisive, and kind all at once. Writing poetry can be a lonely business; working on this book with everyone at Brick made me feel much less alone.

Poems in this collection previously appeared in *Cactus Heart*, *Potluck*, *Plenitude*, *Glass Buffalo*, *The Maynard*, *Arc Poetry*, *Cascadia Review*, and *Event*. Thank you to the editors of each for selecting and supporting my work. Particular thanks to *Glass Buffalo* editor Matthew Stepanic for championing my poem "Lupo Mannaro," which was the 2020 Poetry Gold Winner in the Alberta Magazine Awards. Some of the poems in this collection previously appeared in the chapbook *Shapeshifters*, published by Rahila's Ghost Press; working with the wonderful team at that press, including editor Adèle Barclay, was a bright highlight of 2018.

I'm grateful for the support of the Canada Council for the Arts, without which my life would be materially different.

Thank you to the writing teachers who taught me when I was young and impressionable and thus left an indelible mark on both my work and my life: Becky Godwin, Stephanie Bolster, and especially Silvia Knittel, who isn't here anymore to read this, which I really hate.

Alessandra Naccarato helped revive this project when I was about to abandon it, potentially forever; this book wouldn't be here without her clear vision and generous guidance. Leah Horlick gave me loving feedback, reams of practical advice, and the courage to keep going. Geneviève Gagnon read this work with the enthusiasm and energy of our art-obsessed teenage selves, and helped me translate language into image. Generative conversations over the course of many years with Lindsey Massar and Myriam Parent were foundational to the formation of this collection. Ben Joslyn, B. Pietras, and Joel approached every version of these poems with care and fresh insight. Anthony read every single draft of every poem (including the ones that didn't make the cut), watched an excess of old werewolf movies with me, and accompanied me on field visits (i.e. to church!); every aspect of this collection is imbued with his discernment and support. Thank you all for seeing my work both as it is and as it wants to be—and for seeing me the same way.

In many ways, this book is dedicated to the transformative capacity of friendship, which sustains, inspires, and humbles me. Many of these poems started their lives years ago, some decades ago. I'm grateful to all my friends who have enriched and enlivened my life throughout this creative process. I love knowing and being known by you.

With thanks to the imperfect and beautiful spiritual communities I have found a home and a practice in over the last several decades, where magic is made real. It's an honour and a challenge to grow into adulthood in community, and I'm so thankful for all the support, personal and poetical, over the years.

I'm grateful to my family for instilling in me a love of literature, the natural world, and the unknowable from a young age. Thank you for being my family through all the different ages and stages that life brings. Particular thanks to my mother for creating a magical world in which to grow and to my father for supporting my boy band enthusiasm since I was ten years old.

I know my nonna would have been incredibly proud to hold this book in her hands; that knowledge does little to fill the enormous space created by her absence, but I feel her love across the worlds and send this missive back out in love.

Thank you to the ones keeping me dreaming at home—Anthony, Ben, Fayza, and Imaan. Sharing life and poetry with you is my favourite thing.

Estlin McPhee is a writer and librarian who lives on the traditional territories of the Musqueam, Squamish, and Tsleil-Waututh peoples. They hold an MFA in Creative Writing from the University of British Columbia and are the author of the poetry chapbook *Shapeshifters* (Rahila's Ghost Press, 2018). Estlin's writing has appeared in journals across North America; their poem "Lupo Mannaro" was named the Poetry Gold Winner in Alberta's 2020 Magazine Awards. For many years, they co-organized REVERB, a queer reading series in Vancouver. *In Your Nature* is Estlin's debut poetry collection.